The Psalter of John

The Psalter of John

John M. Etheridge

Templegate Publishers
Springfield, Illinois

Templegate Publishers
302 East Adams Street
Springfield, Illinois 62701
(217) 522–3353

ISBN 0-87243-225-4
Library of Congress Catalog Number: 96–61003

Acknowledgements

This little book could not have been written without the support and encouragement of my wife Frances, my daughters, Jacki and Patti, their husbands, Rocky and James and my granddaughters, Elizabeth, Katherine and Claire. Bill and Virginia Dunham were essential with their critique and editing. I would also like to thank my Rector, Ned Bowersox, for his enthusiasm, and for giving *THE PSALTER OF JOHN* its first major exposure. Thank you to you all.

Introduction

Several years ago we attended a week-end conference at the H.E. Butt Foundation camp near Leakey, Texas which was directed by the Rev. Dr. Elizabeth J. Canham who taught us about the Psalter of David. At one point in the conference she challenged us to write a psalm. Now I have had a problem with poetry all my life. I don't understand it, and never thought I would try to write any. However our conference leader made the psalms come alive and I accepted her challenge. Psalm 1 in The Psalter of John is the result and strangely I enjoyed the effort.

This past Lent, as part of my Lenten pledge, I resolved to write one psalm each week (psalms two through seven). I had so much fun I decided to keep going. I had some things to say to my granddaughters (and anyone else who would listen), about our relationship with God and his plan for us. I feel strongly that God's love for us is much stronger than any of us realize. If he can forgive us for the crucifixion of Jesus, there is nothing we can do which is unforgivable, if we but ask him. I think he gave us The Law for our benefit, that by obeying The Law we could experience the joy of the Kingdom of Heaven. By disobeying, we experience Hell.

I would say to my granddaughters (and anyone else who is still with me) — have a look at our relationship with God.

Read one of these psalms each day and spend a moment in thought about what you have read. My hope is they will bring you closer to our God. Writing them certainly has for me.

Corpus Christi, Texas
July 7, 1994

Psalm 1

O Lord, how great is your love for us
Who can comprehend?
Daily we turn our back on you.
We ignore your commandments,
We deny you in our fear and anxiety.
We search for safety in our possessions,
We abuse the body you have given us,
We waste our lives and all your creation.
We hung your son upon the cross,
And yet you love us still.
O Lord, how great is your love for us
Who can comprehend?

Psalm 2

ord my God, where are you
When I need you?
When the dark angel of despair
Commands my whole being,
When all I see is death and worse,
When my mind is filled with woeful thought,
When everything I do results in failure.
O Lord my God, where are you when I need you?
You are where you always are,
Right beside me.
I have only to reach out and call your name
And you will be there.
You have never been gone,
I have lost sight of you.
I have forgotten your promise to me,
Never to leave me alone.
To be with me to the end of the age,
To bring me peace.
O Lord my God, you are there
When I need you.

Psalm 3

I was awake before you created this day,
It was very dark.
The moon was gone, the stars gave little light,
It was very dark and I was alone.
Somewhere a coyote announced that he was awake,
A songbird called out and was answered by a friend.
Soon there were sounds of life all around me.
It was very dark and I was not alone.
In the east there appeared a fine line of gray
Where the sky met the earth.
The gray line grew wider, and then changed to pink,
And I knew you were here and about to create a new day.
The coyote and songbird were joined by many others,
Joyfully proclaiming your new creation.
The pink sky gave way to a brilliant orange,
and there was light in the land again.
Next came the best of all, the source of light appeared.
A huge orange ball of fire, one of your greatest creations.
It spread its light and warmth far and wide,
The new day was here and all your creatures rejoiced.
O Lord my God, how great you are.
The whole earth sings your praises.
When I look at your creation

I tremble with joy and praise.
I know you are my Lord and Savior,
And I rejoice. I am not alone.

Psalm 4

ord Jesus, when I am asked,
"At what moment do you feel
Closest to Christ?"
My first thought is at a time like this
When I am with you in prayer.
Yet there are other times just as close,
But I don't see you until later.
There are times when I struggle with an impossible problem
And suddenly the answer is there,
And I congratulate myself on such a brilliant decision.
Then I hear a soft voice saying "Praise the Lord."
Now that is close, like the times at worship
When I read Holy Scripture,
Or at the Eucharist when I pass the Cup.
Or when in a conflict I reach the end of my patience
And suddenly I feel relief,
I know you are there, I feel your presence.
At what moment do I feel closest to you?
The moment I need you most.
O Lord Jesus, how I thank you
For your constant presence.

Psalm 5

lmighty Lord, your design of the body you
Gave us is beyond description,
It is so fantastic.
The neuromuscular function is pure genius,
As is the skeletal structure.
The use of a chemical reaction to transmit a nerve impulse
Could only be devised by you.
Your greatness is seen in your entire creation,
And while no human can approach your ability,
And I shudder when I make this statement,
I have a small complaint about the design.
It seems to me that with your genius
You could have created a different relationship
Between the foods that taste so good
And the foods that are good for us.
Or maybe if you had just made the foods that are bad for us
Taste as bad as they are for us.
If only butter tasted a little like lard,
And fried foods tasted like cardboard
It would be a little easier to take better care
Of this wonderful body you created for us.
It would have been easy for you to make
Broccoli taste like rich chocolate ice cream

Or even broiled skinless chicken
Taste like a charbroiled heavy beef steak.
Don't think I am not grateful
For all you have given us,
Because I thank you before every meal
For the wonderful gift of nourishment
That you provide for us. It is just my weakness
That makes me want an easier road to health.
I thank you for butter and beef steak and chocolate and wine
I just wish they were as good for me as they taste.

Psalm 6

Lord my God, creator of the universe
And everything in it
Your creative ability is never demonstrated
Better than in your creation of friends.
Long before you came to earth as our Lord Jesus
Scripture tells us of many friendships
Which demonstrate the value of this relationship
And how it can enrich our lives.
But then as Jesus you offered friendship
To your apostles and through them to us.
Furthermore as your friend I have learned
To develop friendships with others,
And being a friend to another person
I can see you in them, and they can see you in me.
The joys of friendship are unlimited.
They constantly warm my heart.
The special friendship of a man and woman
Who choose to spend their life together,
Is probably the greatest of all your creations,
Offering the opportunity to create new life,
That new life creating a family where
Your love and friendship can be shared and taught.

I have experienced this in my family, Lord,
And rejoice and thank you daily for this gift.
O Lord my God, creator of the universe
and everything in it,
I thank you and praise you for all your gifts,
But especially for the gift of friendship.

Psalm 7

ow great you are, O Lord.
You have created matter to come together
To form this island in the ocean of space.
You have made it habitable for these your
Creatures.
I have seen your power in the raging ocean
When you made the wind blow the sea into sixty -foot waves.
Waves that crushed everything in their path,
And destroyed mighty man-made ships.
I have felt your power when your Spirit comes
And invades your creatures
To make them strong and capable of fantastic
Accomplishments beyond their abilities,
To heal a broken heart or mend a fractured body.
To cool a raging fever, or stop a lethal hemorrhage.
Your power is without limit, it is incomprehensible.
I tremble when I consider
That I can stand in your presence and not be consumed,
I can talk to you and you hear me.
O Lord my God, how great you are,
Who can comprehend?

Psalm 8

Son of God, Lord Jesus, how can we
Understand your words? They are hard.
Your apostle Mark quotes you: "He who
Would follow me will leave self behind."
How can I do this?
How can I be that unselfish?
Since I was a tiny baby there has been
A force in me driving from within to seek
What is best for me, to look out for myself.
A force so strong that I must struggle to avoid
Taking the biggest share or getting the best seat.
If I must struggle with minor decisions like those
How am I to handle the major problems?
How can I rid myself of this demon?
How can I leave self behind?
You promised to be with me at all times, but
Why don't I feel your presence before
I make a selfish decision, before I place myself first?
Must I learn to seek you out before committing myself?
Must I do all the work? Lord Jesus, Son of God
Your words are hard. How can we understand?

Psalm 9

reator God, Lord of the universe and
Everything in it,
How great you are.
The wonders of your creation are beyond
Imagination;
When I consider what you have done, I tremble.
But of all your creation I have seen so far
Your greatest achievement was when you created girls.
You made them as soft as the finest down,
And as hard as the strongest steel.
You made them tender, loving, and gentle,
Yet they can withstand the worst the world can give.
You made them funny, illogical and capricious.
But capable of outstanding wisdom.
In addition to all this, you made them pleasant to look at
And exciting to hold close.
They are wise enough to let men be men,
But function very well when the men are gone.
Yes Lord, of all your creation I have seen
The greatest yet are girls.

Psalm 10

ord God,
Your genius is never better demonstrated than
In the design of the human body. It is a wonder
Beyond belief. A magnificent example of your
Creativity.
Today I saw a man without a hand. The hand you gave him
Had been replaced with a metal device,
A metal device made by man. It looked so inadequate.
Granted it was rather ingenious in itself,
But so extremely awkward when compared
To your original design.
What a wonderful thing you did when you
Designed the thumb to be able to oppose
The other four fingers of that hand, and so to
Hold a scalpel, a paint brush, or a pen,
A switchblade, revolver or Uzi.
Who but you would have thought to design the
Wrist to rotate through one hundred eighty degrees,
And at the same time flex and extend
And medially and laterally bend,
All of which makes it capable of a multitude of
Creative as well as destructive acts?
The hand I saw, the man-made hand,

Was crude and a poor substitute,
But it made me think of what a wonder
The God-given hand is.
Lord God, creator of the universe,
May my hands glorify you.

Psalm 11

Lord God of time and place, orchestrator
Of our Life, I have witnessed again
The miracle of your Genius.
Yesterday I looked out and saw nothing save
Brown grass, bare ground, and leafless trees.
The tree limbs, bare and fruitless reached
Up high to a dark gray sky.
I had the feeling that winter would never end,
That I never again would see the sun.
Then today it happened as you promised.
I saw threading up through the barren brown earth
Little green blades of grain in uniform rows,
Planted there in faith and hope,
That once again the warmth and rain would come
And start the life cycle once more.
I looked forward in anticipation to
The day when the fields would be blanketed
With green as far as I could see; the tree limbs
Covered with leaves and early signs of buds.
I also know that soon there will be a full moon,
Soon we will gather in a darkened church
To hear again of your long loving relationship with us,
And how time and again we have disappointed you.

Then how you have called us back to offer us another plan,
Only to have us distort it and use it to glorify ourselves.
Then you sent your greatest gift of all, your only Son,
To show us how we could experience your kingdom
In this life if we would follow his interpretation of your law.
But we knew better, rejected him, we hung him on the tree.
It must have grieved you mightily; your love never faltered.
In three days you gave him back to us, glorified by you.
That was nearly two thousand years ago, and while
Today we celebrate your great gift,
We still don't understand why you love us so much.
Why again and again you reach out to us to save us.
But we continue to rejoice in and celebrate this happening,
Hoping to please you and one day to understand.
Like the return of the green to the fields and trees,
We are renewed in faith and hope by this celebration.
And even though we don't completely understand
Your love for us, we rejoice in it and thank you for it.
Thank you, Lord God, for your many gifts, but most of all
Thank you for your Son, our Lord Jesus the Christ.

Psalm 12

Lord God of life and death, how great it is to
Know you.
Yesterday I sat with a man as he died.
I held his hand as he struggled to force a little
More air into his diseased lungs.
He grasped my hand and strained the respiratory
Muscles in his chest and neck
In order to find a little more life-giving oxygen,
Only ultimately to fail, and gradually succumb.
I spoke to you then as I prayed for him.
I said comforting words to the family,
Then I left that place. I went back into the other world
Where there was joy and laughter.
Where they didn't feel the pain of sorrow,
Where I was among the living.
I did the work you have given me to do,
Listening, healing, comforting, promising.
But as I went about my work I felt that tight grip
On my hand. The grip of the dead.
It reminded me that I too will die and my family will grieve
And I am sad.
But not for long because I know you,
And I know you have a plan for me.

And I know you will comfort my family and friends,
Because they know you also.
I wonder if the dead man knew you,
I pray that he did.

Psalm 13

ord God, creator of everything we experience,
You have surrounded us with beauty.
Everywhere we look we see beauty in the world
You have made for us.
The trees, the flowers, the green grass at our
Fingertips,
The ocean, the mountains, the fertile plains,
All of this you have made for our pleasure and enjoyment.
Moreover you have given us the gift of creativity.
With the talent you have given us we are able to
Paint pictures, sculpt figures, write drama,
Novels, and poetry, act, sing, and play instruments of music.
You also gave us the ability to enjoy these gifts.
More than that, you gave us the ability to enjoy
The creations of other talented people.
In fact, even those of us who have little talent can
Enjoy the genius of the masters and near masters.
I would like to thank you for those of your children
Who are able to write music.
Music that can calm a troubled mind,
Heal a wounded spirit, inspire us to greatness,
Is a gift from you which is among the greatest
Of all your wonderful gifts.

Thank you, Lord God, for all you have done for us,
And thank you especially for the gift of music.

Psalm 14

Lord God, creator of the universe and
Supreme healer, hear my prayer.
Today I told a friend of mine
That he had cancer.
We cried.
The malignant growth had been silent
Until it was too late for medical science to help.
True, we can slow its growth and ease the pain,
But only you can heal him.
I understand you have many ways of healing,
And some only you understand.
However my friend would like to be rid
Of this death-rendering tumor.
You know his wife and children,
They are your devoted followers.
They will never turn their back on you,
Even if he is healed by death.
They need him desperately and would be most grateful
If he were restored to health.
Lord, I know you hear my prayer,
And I know your decision will be best for all.
Lord God, magnificent healer of the sick and wounded,
Heal my friend.

Psalm 15

lmighty God, magnificent architect
Of the human
Form and physiology,
I have praised your creativity before, and
never cease to wonder at your genius.
The phenomenon of extracting energy from
Ingested complex chemical compounds,
Is without question miraculous, and could
Only have been accomplished by you.
You gave our body power to manufacture the
Chemicals necessary for this conversion,
And not only that, you devised a way to recover
The waste products to be used again.
In this awesome process, and it frightens me to
Mention this, there is one flaw.
The digestive process creates energy and
Raw products for the body's use.
This is good and is handled forthrightly,
However it also creates gas which in some of us
Is not handled well at all. In fact it can
Cause near disaster in some.
Daily I am confronted by people whose only
Problem is caused by this gas.

They complain of pain and bloating, abdominal distention,
Their clothes don't fit, and it disturbs their sleep.
Moreover, they are embarrassed at social functions
When their intestines rumble with turmoil,
Making their companions uncomfortable and anxious,
Fearing what might be coming next.
I know Lord that the main cause of the problem
Is improper diet, and abstinence from exercise.
However it seems to me you could make a minor
Adjustment which would solve the problem.
Perhaps a gas-dissolving enzyme or maybe
An intestinal transudate could absorb the gas.
I know you are busy, Lord, and you may not
Have time to deal with this soon.
You have a lot more important problems to solve
And their visits *are* covered by Medicare.

Psalm 16

aster planner and Lord,
I have a problem and need your help.
I understand you are looking
To include everyone
In your kingdom, excluding no one.
And I understand that you expect us who know you
To introduce you to those who don't know you.
Yet there are those who know you, or at least
Have been introduced to you,
That don't follow you or confess you as their God.
Some have even been baptized.
The behavior and life style of some of them
Must surely sadden you.
Yet there are some whose behavior and life style
Must fill your heart with joy.
I have such a friend. He is honest, kind, gentle,
Loving, fair, a faithful husband and father.
Surely he is filled with your grace because
I find you in his very being.
Moreover you give the gift of creativity and
Understanding to professed nonbelievers.
Does it not matter if we do not confess you
And surrender our lives to you?

I think not. I feel the call to worship you
Is another gift from you to which I must respond.
Just as I must speak to you daily and
Share the love you have for me.
It must be that you can invade the minds and bodies
Of even those who don't know you,
And use them for your purpose to comfort and
Benefit those who are yours.
I have much to learn, Lord, please
Don't give up on me.

Psalm 17

mighty God, source of all power and might,
How wonderful and generous of you
To share that power with us, your created.
How wonderful indeed.
With that power we have the ability to
Think, to plan, to create, to build and to control.
We have learned to send messages instantly.
To travel to the moon, and soon beyond.
We have developed wonderful machines
To heal and keep the dying alive.
We have also learned how to destroy life
Quickly and efficiently with our machines.
It seems that sometimes we think the power you
Have given us makes us gods, and we forget you.
What a magnificent gift you have given us
And we have misused it.
Have mercy on us, have mercy on us, have mercy on us,
Hear my prayer.

Psalm 18

Giver of life to all that live, how great you are.
O Lord my God, creator of all there is,
You have created us in such a way that
We will never understand
Everything about us.
We have learned a great deal about our bodies
And our minds but far from everything.
There is this person inside me whom
I have known for years as me.
As I have grown older, experienced many things,
I have seen this person change.
The changes are many and great and
Hopefully for the better, but I
Still recognize this person inside me
As the person I started with.
This morning I looked in the mirror
And saw an old man looking back.
A stranger looking back at me,
Not the person I have known all these years.
It makes me think you have made part
Of us to last forever and part to wear out.

Lord, you know how I feel about this wonderful body you
Have given us. It is great.
But knowing what I do about me,
I think you are keeping the best part.

Psalm 19

Jesus Christ, Son of God, have mercy
On me, a sinner.
I have known forever of your admonition
To love one another.
I know your mission on earth was
To show us how to love each other.
You demonstrated in your life that it is
Humanly possible to love everybody.
Try as hard as I can, it has been impossible
For me to love those who hate you.
I can't love the child abuser, the wife beater,
The habitual criminal or social outcast.
But worse than that, there are people who
Because of their haircut or life style
Or personal weakness, hard as I try
I cannot love.
Oh, because of your admonition I behave
As if I love them. They never know.
I have learned that if I look for you in them
I can behave lovingly toward them.

They don't feel my unlove. They are not hurt.
Only I feel the pain of separation.
Jesus Christ, Son of God, have mercy
On me, a sinner.

Psalm 20

on of God, Lord Jesus, Savior of the world,
We talked recently about my problem,
The problem of my inability to love everybody.
I have learned something about me.
Remember I told you that if I looked for you
In those unlovables, I could behave as if
I loved them.
The strangest thing has happened. I have found
The longer I am around them,
The less I notice the offensive things
That made them unlovable to me.
Now I still abhor the traits and life style which
Alienated me in the first place,
But in separating the person from the life style,
I can love the person, and abhor the life style.
This does not come easy, Lord. I must work
At it all the time. I cannot relax.
If you were not here, I could not do it at all.
Lord Jesus, have mercy on me, a sinner.

Psalm 21

eavenly Father, supreme healer
Of the universe,
I have been sick, uncommonly sick.
My body was racked with fever, my bones
Ached beyond belief, I trembled with chills.
Massive fatigue engulfed my whole being,
I was sick unto death.
I asked you to heal me, and you did.
I praise your name, and thank you for your gift.
Now I feel wonderful again, but I remember
How it felt to be sick, it was miserable.
As I was recovering, and knew that I was going to live
I began to think of some of my
Friends who live with pain and discomfort
Every day, who never feel good.
There are times when they feel better but
They are never free of pain,
They can never say "I feel good."
They can only feel a little better.
Lord God, healer of the universe, hear my prayer,
Heal my friends.
Give them the freedom from pain and travail
That you intend for us all.

Psalm 22

ing of Kings, Lord God, source of
All knowledge and intelligence, help me.
I know you love us because
You have given us
Power and knowledge to control our lives.
You have given us the ability to conquer space,
To transplant body parts, to cure disease.
You have given us the beauty of a sunset,
Wonderful foods to satisfy our hunger,
Loving friends and companions to share your
Many bountiful gifts.
We know you love us very much. Your love should
Make us feel important and superior.
We should feel complete and not need any
Ego-building or self-promoting.
Why then, Lord, do we constantly do and say
Things to improve our image to others?
Why do we often misrepresent the truth in order
To make ourselves look more important?
Why do we not feel important enough just
Being the one you have created and love?
There must be a negative force in us which tends
To disparage the importance of your love.

I hope and pray that force is part of the body
Which is wearing out.
I would not like to think I would keep it forever.
It has no place in your kingdom.

Psalm 23

ou, Heavenly Father, Son, Holy Spirit,
Almighty God,
Are provider of all I need.
You comfort me, love me, feed me,
Protect me from all my enemies.
You guide me in all my action if I will but listen.
You rescue me from my errors in judgment.
When you are with me I am fearless,
Nothing can overcome me.
Many are puzzled and wonder at my confidence,
They don't know your power.
I will prosper and grow stronger all my life
Because I belong to you and will forever.

Psalm 24

y Lord and God, creator
Of everything there is,
Your genius is beyond belief.
When you made male and female
You created maleness and femaleness,
And it was good. Now I am having a problem
And I need your help.
Yesterday I overheard a conversation between
Two charming young ladies,
Who were discussing the relative merits
Of their husbands' cologne.
I was shocked to learn that they would prefer
The maleness of their mates to be altered,
In such a way that they would smell like flowers.
I expressed my concern to them,
And said I thought men should smell like hard work,
Tobacco, whiskey, gasoline, and no more than soap.
They violently disagreed and reaffirmed their
Preference for sweet-smelling men.
Lord, I may have lived too long, things are changing
So fast I cannot keep up.
Help me, Lord, to adjust to the changes that are
Taking place today. I have much more to do.

Psalm 25

Lord God of the universe and
Author of all wisdom,
Help me understand.
I read in the prophet Isaiah that the wicked
Are like a troubled sea that cannot rest.
Moreover there is no peace for the wicked.
Our Lord Jesus says he came to bring us peace,
And I have experienced the peace of being with him.
However I have thought wicked thoughts,
Which with a little philosophical manipulation
I have been able to justify in my mind.
I can build a thesis supported by righteous indignation,
And sound very pious in my presentation.
Yet deep within me I feel that turbulence of the
Troubled sea mentioned in Isaiah.
If you are indeed with me always,
Where do these wicked thoughts come from?
Are they from the evil force that seems to
Reside in me also?
Must we constantly challenge this evilness
With your power of goodness?
How are we to know when we are cleansed of the evil?
Will you calm the troubled sea?

Psalm 26

raised be your name, Lord God,
Author of life and after life.
Yesterday we buried a friend.
Now he is with you.
As we congregated before the procession,
The bishop prayed "Thank you, Lord, for life."
After we had all gathered inside, we prayed,
And heard the Holy Scripture read.
The homilist then said "We are not here to glorify
The dead, but to glorify God."
He also said "God is now rejoicing because he
Has one of his loving children home with him,
And he that we buried is rejoicing too,
To be finally home with God."
It made me think about how wonderful it will be
To be constantly at your side, feeling
Your strength, experiencing your love,
Basking in your protection and care.
Then I remembered Jesus has already offered
This life to us here and now.
We don't have to wait until we die to be with you,

We can be with you, and enjoy all
The comforts of your kingdom if we will have
Faith in our Lord Jesus, and call upon him.
Lord God, thank you for the gift of life
And thank you for our Lord Jesus, the Christ.

Psalm 27

Lord God my creator, Lord Jesus my savior,
Lord Holy Spirit my comforter,
I need your help.
When I am in trouble,
When my enemies descend on me,
And surround me on every side,
And I can see my very life slipping away,
I can reach out to you, and you are there.
You are there to comfort me, to heal me,
To make me strong, to overcome my foes.
I know you will be there to save me,
I need only to call your name and you are there.
If I have this confidence in you when I am troubled,
Why do I feel this distance between us when I
Am not troubled?
When things are going smoothly in my life,
When my problems are solved, my enemies gone,
Why do I congratulate myself for my wisdom,
My good judgment, my ability and skill?
Why do I neglect my prayer time with you,
That life-giving period each day,
That supplies the power I need to be the person
You have created and saved?

Why do I so easily forget my troubled times,
When you have delivered me from the jaws of death,
When you have calmed the troubled waters
That would have inundated me?
Is my love for you so shallow that I only feel
It when I need you? I hope not.
Lord, I pray you will give me the power to
Resist the feeling of self-sufficiency
Which conceals from me my need for you,
My life-giving source of power.
Help me remember you are the source of all of
My joy, all of my peace, and my freedom.
Thank you, Lord, for all you have done for me,
And have mercy on me, a sinner.

Psalm 28

I have discovered something, O Lord God,
Creator of the mystery of life.
Yesterday a friend praised me
For something I had done.
I thanked him kindly and went on my way.
Then I noticed a feeling come over me
Which was wonderful. I was changed.
The weather was no longer unbearably hot,
The traffic was no longer intolerable.
The pain in my body was replaced with
A feeling of euphoria such as I have seldom known.
I looked forward to my work ahead with joy,
I knew no fear, no task was too hard.
My computer was a friend to help me,
Not a demon planning my demise.
Then I thought, this is the state that God
Has planned for us, this is heaven.
I have experienced a taste of what you want
Our life to be all the time,
And what we can look forward to in the
Greater life with you in heaven.

All it took to initiate this great feeling
Was a few words of approval from my friend.
Thank you, Lord God, for my friend and
Thank you for this glimpse of paradise.

Psalm 29

ow wonderful are your Holy Scriptures,
Lord God of wisdom and all creation.
Today I read in the gospel of John
A question of Peter's which made me think.
In response to your question
About his loyalty,
He asked "Lord to whom shall we go?"
From time to time I have mentally played with
The concept of your not being real.
I considered in my mind what my life would
Be like without you.
I pictured my motivation, my goals, my driving force.
Where would my strength come from?
What hope would I have depending on my own
Resources for my drive?
I don't play this game very long, Lord.
The picture I see is very unpleasant.
I would find life very lonely without you,
And very incomplete.
I saw no joy, no hope, no comfort,
Only fear and despair.

Peter was right. Where can I go without you?
Without you I am nothing.
Lord God, creator, Lord Jesus, savior,
Holy Spirit, comforter,
Stay close to me.

Psalm 30

ord God, grantor of every perfect gift,
How can I express my gratitude?
Last Sunday at worship we sang
"Rejoice, give thanks and sing."
For the rest of a peaceful sleep,
I rejoice, give thanks and sing.
For the love of a devoted spouse,
For the joy of loving children,
For the excitement of precious grandchildren,
I rejoice, give thanks and sing.
For a vocation that is helpful, rewarding and fun,
For fellow workers who are loyal, accomplished
And trustworthy, who make my task easy,
I rejoice, give thanks and sing.
For friends who share my love for you,
And for some who don't, yet.
For good food, red wine and single malt scotch,
And time to share it with friends and family,
For the mystery of life, and my closeness to you,
I rejoice, give thanks and sing. Alleluia.

Psalm 31

Father in heaven, Lord God, how great you are.
You know our needs and our weakness,
And you have supplied everything for us
Before we recognize our requirements.
You have supplied the nourishment our bodies
Require, and have shown us how to use them.
You know our need to be protected from the elements,
And have provided shelter.
Our fragile personalities need love and acceptance,
And you have given us friends to support us.
But most of all you knew we could not or
Would not obey your law, so you
Sent us Jesus, to show us how to live and love you.
Then he died on the cross for our sin.
Not only died for us, but while hanging on the cross,
He prayed that you forgive us, and you have.
O God our father, how great you are,
O God our father, how great you are.

Psalm 32

Lord my God and provider of all I possess,
How great is your generosity.
Daily I thank you for all you have given me.
I know everything comes from you.
Yesterday I heard a man ask,
"Would you still
Love God if you lost all your possessions?"
I was startled, and I began to think. How would
I feel losing everything I own?
Although I say everything comes from you, I take
Great pride in all I have collected and accomplished.
I would feel devastated, cursed and filled with despair.
My depression would be complete.
I would be filled with anger and would cry out
"Life is not fair."
But I hope and pray that I would not blame you.
You are my very source of hope.
Only you can rescue me from my despair. Only
You can renew my desire to live.
And live I must to serve you, to glorify you,
To bring your love to those who know you and
Those who don't.
The life you have given us is a wonderful gift.

It is full of much pleasure and joy.
At times we tend to forget the pleasure and joy
Is an extra and not the gift.
O Lord my God, help me keep my eyes on you,
And your gifts in proper perspective.

Psalm 33

ource of all knowledge and truth,
O Lord our God,
I praise your holy name.
We were reading in The Wisdom of Solomon,
From your Holy Scriptures,
When I suddenly realized that we could be
Reading from today's newspaper.
The situations described in scripture were
The same things that are happening today.
We have ignored your teaching, we ridicule
Your plan for us, we deride your presence.
We pay no heed to your natural law, we dismiss
Your law of life as meaningless.
As the people of old, we look to our own pleasure
And trample on the needs of others.
We have learned nothing from history.
We behave as if history started with us.
It is good that you have a forgiving nature.
It is good that you love us, sinners that we are.
Thank you, Lord God, for your wonderful love.
Have mercy on us.

Psalm 34

Lord Jesus Christ, son of God,
Savior of all mankind,
We need your help.
I heard a popular song today and
I was troubled by the lyrics.
The soloist asked "If I fall in love with you,
How can I know you will love me too?"
He did not want to risk his love until he could be
Sure his love would be returned.
The pain would be too great for him to find
Himself not loved in return.
These words made me wonder how you must feel
Having given your life for us because you loved us,
Knowing full well that many of us would never
Return that love,
Knowing that some would reject you without
Even knowing what you offer us,
Knowing that many would embrace you only because
Being yours offers them respectability.
Your love for us is beyond our understanding,
It is greater than anything we know.
Lord Jesus, we know little of your love
We need your help.

Psalm 35

Architect of humanity and
Lord God of all creation,
How great you are.
Yesterday I looked inside a knee joint again
And praised your holy name.
The design is spellbinding. The structure is
Outstanding. The function is unbelievable.
Muscles, tendons, cartilage and bone you have
Arranged to support, and carry our body
As we stand, walk, run, dance, kneel and climb,
Never failing in a lifetime of normal use.
I looked down on a joint that had been abused,
And as we cut away the damaged tissue,
I praised your name again. Even though we
Destroy the body you have given us,
You have led us to learn how to repair and
Replace that which we have destroyed.
As we replaced the damaged articular surface,
I thanked you again and again,
Knowing full well that the resulting joint would
Fall far short of the original design,
But also knowing the joint would function much
Better than it had. Pain was relieved.

Thank you, Lord God, for the body you have given us.
And thank you for being in our lives,
For making your presence known to us,
And using us to do your work and will.

Psalm 36

ow can we know you,
Lord God of understanding and love?
Last Sunday when we were gathered for
Worship the celebrant
Opened with the familiar words,
"Blessed be God: Father, Son and Holy Spirit."
We responded: "And blessed be his kingdom,
Now and Forever."
With that we were launched into the ancient
Ritual inaugurated by our Lord Jesus the Christ,
The celebration he left us in order that we
Might be part of him, and he of us.
We gathered as believers, nonbelievers but obedient,
And want-to-be-believers.
We were contaminated by and felt uneasy because of
The evil within each of us.
We suffered from greed, envy, hate, distrust,
Avarice, gluttony, and self-centeredness.
We went hopefully through the ritual, praying
That the corporate good in us
Would outweigh the corporate evil in us and
We would be acceptable in your sight.
If we but realized how much you love us,

We would be rejoicing and singing,
Not fearing your wrath, or doubting your existence.
We would be joy-filled in your presence.
We would long to share this wonderful feeling
With everyone who doesn't know you.
Lord God of understanding and love
We need your help.

Psalm 37

ven some of your most faithful are suffering,
Lord God of understanding and all creation.
I know of a man, devoted to you for years,
A teacher, an evangelist, a tither and more,
An eager servant in his
Community of believers,
Who yet did not feel blessed by his church.
He was a hard and joyful worker at any task,
And always did a praiseworthy job.
He worshiped daily, privately during the week,
And with all of us on Sunday.
He accomplished great things for your kingdom,
Yet never felt the approval of his fellow worshipers.
You have made us very fragile and sensitive,
And created in us needs we don't understand.
We need the love, acceptance, and approval
Of those with whom we live, work, and play.
Moreover we must recognize that need in others,
And fulfill that need with our love, acceptance and approval.
In order to do that, we must listen to that spark of you
That lives within us, and respond to it.
O Lord of Creation and Understanding help us
Hear your voice when you speak; help us spread your love.

Psalm 38

esus, Lord and savior of the world and all mankind,
Help me know what to ask of you.
Today we read from Holy Scripture in Mark
Your question to Bartimaeus
"What do you want me to do for you?"
And I felt you were asking me.
My first prayer when I come in your presence
Is always one of thanksgiving.
You have already done so much for me
I hesitate to ask for more.
Yet there are always friends and family members
For whom I pray, asking for your blessing and healing.
I recite the prayer you taught us each morning and night,
Although I often don't listen to what I am saying.
I have the feeling you want me to ask you
Something else, something more important;
Ask you for something which would make me
More faithful, more productive for you,
Something which would make me grow spiritually and to be
More like the person you would have me be.

I will need your help, Lord Jesus. Without it I will
Never hear your voice, never have the strength.
Lord Jesus, savior of the world and all mankind,
Help me know what to ask of you.

Psalm 39

hank you, Lord God our creator,
Lord Jesus our savior,
Lord Holy Spirit our comforter, thank you.
Thank you for your great gift of relationships,
Thank you for adopting us as your children.
I was thinking about all the things which give me joy,
My possessions, my home, my vocation, my family,
And the question came to me "which is the greatest,
Which gives me the maximum joy?"
I asked myself "Which would I be least willing to lose?"
"Which could I not do without?"
I didn't ponder long. Without my family I
Would have no joy at all. I would despair.
Then I realized that you created the love we
Share in family relationships and you
Invite us to join you in a relationship in which
You supply all the love, protection and comfort.
It is the love you give us which makes possible
The joy we can experience in our love for others.
The greatest thing in life is knowing you and
Being part of your family.
Lord God our creator, Lord Jesus our savior, Lord
Holy Spirit our comforter, thank you.

Psalm 40

esterday, Lord our God,
Healer of all the ills of mankind,
I witnessed your genius again.
My friend had an obstruction in a
Main artery to her brain.
Her brain was starved for life-giving blood.
She had suffered a light stroke which left one side
Weak, and frightened all of us.
As I looked on, the surgeon skillfully opened the skin,
And carefully dissected down to the obstruction.
The great artery was opened, the obstruction removed,
And the artery closed again.
I was once more aware of your genius in design,
And I praised your name.
The wall of this major vessel was less than a millimeter
In thickness, yet withstood years of constant
Pounding without wearing out. Moreover it has the
Ability to heal itself after being opened and closed.
Now the blood is flowing rapidly again, taking
Essential oxygen and food to the brain.
My friend will soon be going home. Her body will
Soon be whole, she will be healed.

Thank you, Lord God, for your healing grace,
Your gift of love, knowledge, and skill.
I praise your holy name and thank you for the
Wonderful body you designed for us.

Psalm 41

was at worship today, O Lord,
And the music was grand.
We sang songs of praise and it was beautiful.
As I read the words of the hymns I was overcome
With their eloquence in your praise.
When the hymn ended with "Alleluia, Alleluia, Alleluia"
I sang out with joy and enthusiasm.
Then I felt myself sink into a pit of despair.
Deep gloom surrounded and engulfed me.
I felt bad that my words were not as eloquent
In praise as those of the hymn.
I am unable to verbalize my feelings and
Express my love and wonder with words.
My words will never do justice to the way I feel,
But I trust you know how I feel in my heart.
I must use someone else's words at worship but
When I explode with "YES" or "ALL RIGHT"
You will know how I feel, and that I am doing the best I can.
O Lord, how can I know how great you are?

Psalm 42

ow wonderful is the life you have given us,
Lord God, creator of all living things.
I want to thank you Lord for all my life,
But especially this particular time in my life.
It is great being more of a spectator
Than a planner; being an observer,
Rather than a decision-maker. I know well my
Life is in your hands.
It is totally liberating when it is not so important
To be "right," to have the biggest or best.
It is good to have time to really listen to my friends
And talk to you.
It makes we wonder if I might have enjoyed
These blessings sooner,
If I had but adopted this attitude sooner.
I wonder.
In any event I am enjoying it now and
I thank you for it.
Lord God, creator of all living things,
How wonderful the life you have given us.

Psalm 43

oday is the last day in the liturgical year
When we celebrate Christ the King.
The preacher asked "Who is your king?"
Then he enumerated the
Earthly kings we follow.
They included pretension, conformity and power
As the most prevalent and devastating.
It made me think of the areas in my life
That separate me from you.
It made me know again how much you love us;
How much you will tolerate.
My earthly kings cannot give me the comfort
That you give me.
Your love and support is so much greater
And long-lasting. It is forever.
Time after time I chase after the now-pleasures,
And time after time you wait patiently for
My return.
Your love is beyond understanding.
Jesus Christ, Son of God, have mercy on me.

Psalm 44

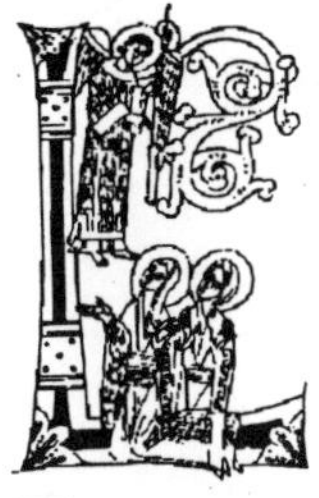

ord Jesus, Son of God,
Today I felt very close to you
And it was nice.
The little girl stirred in her sleep,
Struggled free of
The covers, and stood in her bed.
I approached and she held out her arms to me and
I remembered the many times I had experienced
This before.
As I picked her up I was flooded with memories.
It was nice.
We walked into another room, she put her head
On my shoulder and dozed.
After much too short a time she again struggled
To awaken and
Soon she was through with my protective arms.
She climbed down full of life.
At last free from the prison of sleep, she trotted off,
Ready to face the adventures of this day.
Lord Jesus, Son of God, thank you for little girls
And for memories.

Psalm 45

our greatness, Lord God our King,
Is seen in all you have made.
Yet all the psalms, songs and
Prayers in the world
Don't begin to praise you enough.
Your design of all living things required a
Genius beyond description.
You made all living creatures interdependent,
Then produced an environment in which they
Could flourish.
You gave them an instinct to survive, and built into
Them the ability to do it.
Then in your greatest design you placed the
Intelligence to know you, and
Wonder of wonders, you gave us the freedom
To deny your existence.
Yet into each of us you placed a burning desire
To know you and be with you.
We try to satisfy that desire with possessions,
Prestige and power.
But they all fall short. They are so transient.
They cannot replace you.
You must love us very much, beyond our understanding

To tolerate the things we do to be
more powerful than you.
Lord God our King, your greatness
Is seen in all you have made.
Help me make you known in all the world.

Psalm 46

o one, Lord God, creator of mankind and all
The world, can tell us how great you are.
Your genius has been praised
Generation after generation.
I have told of your majesty from my youth.
There is no one with your creative power.
Having said all that, and knowing what you must
Think of complainers, I have a complaint.
Your creation of mankind in your image was a
Stroke of divine genius, but there is one flaw.
You created in us a spirit, power or instinct
That causes us, immediately on hearing a law, to
Start calculating how we might avoid it or
Turn it to our advantage.
We never look at it as something that might
Be good for us.
We never consider that the law might protect us
From injury and harm.
We assume that it will infringe on our individual rights
And usurp our freedom.
There is even a group of us that has become so
Skilled in the process, they have become a profession.
This trait makes it hard to follow your recommended

Life style, and it disrupts domestic tranquility.
Is this part of the total freedom you have given us?
Sometimes freedom is hard to live with.
Lord God, creator and protector, stay close,
Protect us from ourselves.

Psalm 47

raised be your holy name,
Lord God of the universe, creator of all there is.
We are now in the season of Advent and are
Relearning the history of your love for us.
It is exciting to hear again the stories
In Holy Scripture
That tell how you wooed us and sought our love.
One has only to read this account to know that
You love us with a passion.
Again and again we have accepted your deliverance,
And promised to remain true to you forever,
Only to return to our selfish ways as soon as
Freedom was recognized.
How can you love us this much, Lord?
What is there about us that so attracts you?
If you can love us so, why can't we love each other?
Why can't we see in each other what you see in us?
Maybe this Advent we will learn more about your love.
I pray that we will.

Psalm 48

Lord God Almighty, grantor of
The most perfect gift,
The anniversary of your greatest
Gift is upon us;
Second in glory only to the resurrection
Of our Lord Jesus,
The celebration of his incarnation.
Believers, doubters, and nonbelievers feel the
Excitement of your spirit within them.
The most self-centered and greedy cannot escape
The feeling of joy your spirit brings.
Even those who have never heard of you
Are caught up in the excitement.
Many take advantage of the feeling abroad
And add to their own accumulation of treasure.
But even knowing this the celebrants forgive
Them in their joy and happiness.
Tragedies occur and are felt more deeply
And remembered longer, but the
Overall feeling is one of an expanding vision
Of hope which your spirit brings.
Is this a picture of what you have
In store for us, O Lord?

Or is this a taste of the sweetness our life
Could be if we were closer to you?
Lord have mercy on us. Christ have mercy on us.
Lord have mercy on us.

Psalm 49

ord Jesus Christ, Son of God,
Have mercy
On me, a sinner.
I have prayed this prayer many times and
Never more intensely than now.
In my psalter, in my ignorance, and
Naivete, I may have offended you.
Please know that was not my intention
And I pray you have not been offended.
My knowledge of you tells me that if you still
Love us after what we did on Good Friday,
There is nothing we can do which will make
You abandon us.
I understand we can turn our backs on you,
But you will never abandon us.
It seems to me that all your gifts for us
Are meant to make our life here
As joyful as in your kingdom. In fact your plan
Is to establish your kingdom here.
And the laws you gave us were for that purpose.
They were to make our life better.
We are not to obey your law to please you,
Rather, it is for our benefit,

To give us the life you want for us.
What a wonderful thing you have done for us.
Lord Jesus, Son of God, have mercy on me,
A sinner.

Psalm 50

uthor of every perfect gift,
O Lord my God and creator,
I have a problem.
Some of your children, those you love dearly,
Have treated me badly.
Time after time, they rob me of my possessions,
They lie to me and drag me into court.
They accuse me of things I have not done,
And demand retribution.
They ignore contractual promises,
And refuse to give me my due.
They live in big homes, drink fine wine, enjoy the good life,
All at my expense.
I cry out in my despair, and I am not heard.
I am ridiculed and laughed at.
I have no place to go, O Lord, except to you.
You are my refuge, my strength and salvation.
You have saved me in the past. I depend on you.
Hear my prayer.
I have known of your love for ages. I have seen your work
Among your people.
Surely you can help me in my despair,
You can comfort me and save me from my enemies.

Now that they are finished with me, what do I have?
What is there to give me joy?
True, I have never been hungry. I have never slept
In the cold without shelter.
My family is well fed, comfortably clothed.
They are not neglected.
We have loyal friends who support and comfort us.
We have our health.
We know you and your love for us. We feel your
Presence in your Holy Spirit.
We really have more than we can use wisely.
Why am I crying?
Stay close to me Lord. Do not leave me alone.
Without you I would die.

Psalm 51

he celebration of Pentecost is upon us,
Lord our God,
The day in the religious year when ancient and
Modern Israel celebrate the giving of the law.
Followers of Jesus remember
Pentecost as the day
You sent the Holy Spirit and changed their lives.
What a glorious day that must have been.
With flames of fire and rushing winds you
Opened the minds and hearts of men
And our Church was born.
As your gift of baptism makes us members
Of your family, the gift of the Holy Spirit
Equips us with the power to participate
In your ongoing creation as co-creators.
You must love us very much to share with us
Your creative power. How can we ever thank you?
Is it enough to tithe, worship you on Sunday, and
Be kind to our family and friends? I think not.
We must tell the world about your love. We must bring
Back to you those of yours who have strayed.

We must introduce you to those who don't know you.
We must help you with your plan.
Speak, Lord, your servant listens. How may we serve you?
How can we respond to your love?

Psalm 52

ow generous you are, O Lord my God,
How wonderful are your many gifts.
You have surrounded me
With angels all these years
To help me do the work you have given me.
You have supplied me with fellow physicians,
Nurses and technicians, managers, bookkeepers,
Secretaries, and clerks
To provide the day-to-day support which has made
The healing of your people possible.
They have been present constantly and
Have done their work joyfully with
Your love showing through in all their efforts.
My work would be impossible without them.
And now I am about to take leave of them
And I am sad.
I am happy and excited about what is about
To happen, but sad to leave my friends.
I know you have new adventures in store for them,
But I will miss being a part of their life.
I would pray that you hold them close to you,
And show them your love daily.
Guide them when life presents them with

A difficult decision and reward them,
As only you can, with the riches of your kingdom
And the warmth of your presence.
Thank you again, Lord, for the gift of these angels.
I would not have survived without them.

Psalm 53

lessed giver of life, O Lord
My God and creator,
I praise your holy name.
Each morning I am reminded of your wisdom
When I awaken from a restful sleep.
Only you could have designed such a phenomenon
That could refresh and renew our strength and
Replace the energy and enthusiasm dissipated
In the events of yesterday.
How wonderful it is to retire with a mind full of
Unsolved problems and unfinished tasks,
And to have them gently erased and ultimately
Replaced by the unreal world of dreams.
You have designed our body to use this time to
Slow down and be renewed.
Our blood pressure goes down, as does our heart rate.
All our muscles relax, even those in our arteries.
Our body systems slow down and rest.
We are renewed.
When we awaken we are better prepared to face
Those unsolved problems and unfinished tasks.

Sleep is a wonderful gift, O Lord, and demonstrates
Again how much you love us.
Thank you Lord and I praise your holy name forever,
My God and creator.

Psalm 54

ather of all mankind, Lord our God,
How patient and loving you are.
Many of your people
Have heard of you from another
Source, many do not know you at all.
Yet you love us all. You have offered to each
Of us a savior and advocate, Jesus.
You would hope those of us who know you
Would tell those who don't know you about Jesus.
It is such a rich gift, I don't know how we
Can keep it a secret.
We have not done a very good job of going
Out to all the world and sharing your gift.
We are even living in what is known as
The post-Christian era.
One of your children, who searched diligently
For you all his life, was heard to say
"I like this Jesus, but I don't trust
His followers."
That is not a very good reputation to have.
We need to do better.
(I am glad that you will be our judge
And not that man.)

I would pray, Lord, that you would
Open our hearts to your Holy Spirit
That we might be better spreaders of your
Great gift of love and knowledge of Jesus.
Thank you God our creator, Jesus our savior,
Holy Spirit our comforter and teacher.
Thank you a million times and let your
Holy Name be praised.

Psalm 55

Lord our God, who caused all Holy Scripture
To be written, I praise your name.
Today I was reading in Luke about the time
Your disciple asked you to teach them to pray.
You spoke again of the kingdom of God, and
Asked them to pray for its coming.
This caused me to think about the kingdom,
And what the kingdom is like.
You told many stories about the kingdom
Which were vivid and clear, but
They were set in a time unfamiliar to me,
And I find it difficult to fit myself into the picture.
I know that you were talking about relationships
Which can apply to any time or place,
But I am so dominated by my physical situation
I find it difficult to picture myself anywhere
Other than this time and place. Are you telling us
That we can experience the kingdom here and now?
We would need to change many things about the
Way we live and relate to one another.
We must stop making war with other nations
And our neighbors. We must learn to love
One another as Jesus loved us. You have told

Us this before, haven't you, many times?
We are truly blessed that you love us as you do.
What a wonderful God you are.
I pray your kingdom come, and I also pray
That you continue to love and be patient with us.

Psalm 56

y Lord God, creator,
Savior, and comforter,
I need your help.
In my sleep, I was visited by
A terrifying dream,
In which you finally turned your back on your creation.
You surveyed our life style and values and decided
There was no hope for us.
Our greed, selfishness, gluttony, hate, denial of you
Used up all of your love, and you turned away from us.
I awakened in a cold sweat and trembled in fear.
I could not make myself believe it was a dream.
As I went about my work that day I could think
Of nothing else.
The fear that you might no longer love us
Crippled me, I was devastated.
I cried out to you, "Deliver me from this
State of panic."
You heard my call, and as always answered
My prayer.
At worship this morning the processional hymn
Spoke of your never-ending love.
Paul's letter to the Hebrews reminded us of

Jesus' death on the cross.
I heard you say, "If I can forgive you for the
Crucifixion, is there anything I won't forgive you for?"
As I received the blessed elements at Eucharist
I felt relief and joy again.
I thank you, Lord God, and praise your name.
Thank you for your love and answered prayer.

Psalm 57

am the resurrection and the life," saith the Lord,
The all too familiar words said as we gathered
To celebrate the life of one of ours
And one of yours.
The words that create hope and comfort
In the hearts of the believers,
And words that create fear and despair
In the hearts of the nonbelievers.
We gather to celebrate a life that has been
A wonderful example of what you would have us be.
A devoted husband and father, a dedicated physician,
A loyal churchman, and true friend.
A life that will not end this day, but will
Go on in what you have planned for us.
The priest said "We have gathered to thank God
For the life of our friend,
To ask God for help in dealing with his death,
And to hear what he had to say about God."
He is a true believer, Lord, and I know he is now
In your loving arms, where he belongs.

We will miss him, O Lord, but we know we will
Be with him again because of your promise.
Thank you, God, for your never ending love for us.
Remind us daily, that we may grow in faith.

Psalm 58

Lord God of creation and memories,
I praise your holy name.
Last Sunday as I sat
In our nave in contemplation,
I was flooded with memories. Memories of
Important, life-changing events that have
Occurred in this place. And you were always
There, and I thanked you for them.
For over forty years my family and I have
Worshipped and celebrated here.
We have celebrated the Holy Matrimony of both our
Daughters, the Holy Baptism of two
Of our three granddaughters, the Burial service
Of my wife's parents and innumerable
Celebrations of the Holy Eucharist, Morning Prayer,
Funerals of friends, pageants and special events.
I learned to be a Lay Reader and Chalice bearer,
Represented the Vestry, greeted worshipers,
Took up and counted the collection, picked up
Trash in the yard, and cleaned the men's room.
The most important events in my life have
Happened here. I thank you Lord for this place.

Psalm 59

hank you, Lord Jesus,
Son of God, and our savior,
For the prayer you gave us.
I have prayed it many times and it always
Comforts and strengthens me.
Recently it was especially enlightening; I thought
Of many things.
You are *our* father Lord. Not just mine but also
Father to that difficult person at the office.
Also the person who cheated me in a business deal.
You love them just as you love me.
It makes me think you know something about love
That I don't know.
You really are great and your name
Is Holy.
If I knew how to love the way you do,
I too could love everyone as you do.
If everyone knew how to love that way we
Wouldn't have any relationship problems.
You do want this for us, don't you, Lord?
You have given us so much why do I feel anxious
About my material things, my health, my business?
When I think about it in the light of what you

Have already done, it seems greedy to ask
You for more.
But you know my needs, Father, and one of them
Is the constant need to be reassured that
You are still there.
About forgiveness, you know I expect you to forgive
Me in your own loving way, but just as I
Am unable to love the way you do yet, neither can I
Forgive the way you do — yet.
I am working on it but there is something built into
Me which gets in my way.
About temptation — there is something built in me which
Makes me think of myself, my pleasure,
My well being.
I must depend on you to be with me always, because
There is an evil force out to destroy me
By separating me from you. I am counting on you
To overcome this force of evil.
Father when I look about me at your creation
I know how great you are.
When I realize that I am part of your creation,
I am awe-struck.
When I recognize that you have a plan for me
As part of your creation, I am excited
And frightened.

Excited when I think about you, frightened
When I think about me.
I pray that you will help me
Keep my mind on you.

Amen and Amen

Psalm 60

lmighty Lord, our creator
And gracious benefactor,
We, your children, are having trouble.
We are having trouble with one of your gifts.
As great and wonderful as it is,
We don't seem to be able to handle the
Freedom you have given us.
Just like St. Paul, we do those things we
Ought not do, and we avoid
Those things we ought to do, and there is
Truly no health in us. We are a sick people.
We not only go to war with our neighbor nations,
We wage war among ourselves.
We kill each other and have taught our wicked
Ways to our children.
Nightly we watch murder and mayhem as real
And fictional people destroy each other.
We applaud both corporate and personal dishonesty,
And hold in awe the rich and victorious.
We embrace fornication and promiscuity and have
Made love-making a spectator sport.
We are afflicted with a sickness that no human
Physician can successfully treat.

You have given us a healer and savior, Lord,
But we have turned our back on him.
Restore us, Lord, to the healthy state you have
Designed for us. Heal us Lord.

Psalm 61

ord God almighty, creator of all there is,
Your genius is known in all the world.
You have created mankind in such a way
That this wonderful body you have given us
Will do those things that we
Ought to do for a long
Time if we take good care of it.
Unfortunately it will also do those things that we
Ought not do, but for not as long a time.
Time however takes its toll on our body
No matter what we do, and makes those
Things we ought not do less pleasurable
And less gratifying, and those things we
Ought to do more difficult and time consuming,
And it seems we do with less enthusiasm.
However Lord, you have given us some
Pleasures that don't wear out, and continue
To sustain us and bring us joy.
There is nothing more warming than
A glass of fine sherry with a friend
On a cold, damp night.
A well-cooked meal, even with too much fat,
Served with elegance to family and friends,

Will drive away despair and many of the
Pains of aging.
A very dry Martini raised in celebration
With comrades will restore joy to a drab life.
Watching a grandchild grow and learn makes us
Know you are there and concerned for us.
Thank you Lord for all your many gifts,
You do take good care of us.

Psalm 62

ord God, creator of the universe,
And everything that is good
I praise your name, and thank you.
Yesterday was a great day for me,
And I thank you for it.
I was reminded of your constant love and
Ongoing care and support when
Yesterday I was in the presence of one of yours
Who has provided for one of my needs for forty years.
His faithfulness and concern for me
Must have come from you.
We reminisced about our long-standing relationship
Which gave me the warm feeling
Which I have come to recognize comes
From being in your presence.
It was obvious that everyone in the room felt
The excitement and power in the encounter.
The warmth stayed with me long after I left the place
And colored my entire day.
Thank you Lord for loyal, long time friends,
And thank you, Lord, for Red, my barber.

Psalm 63

Come, Lord Jesus, sit with me for a spell and
Let me experience your presence.
Come, Lord Jesus, be known to me,
Fill my consciousness with your being.
Restore in me the security I have known
When you are near me.
Walk with me to our secret place,
And tell me of God's love again.
Stay with me and hear me out.
I am lost without you.
I know you have experienced all the hurts
I have felt. You have suffered more than I.
Being in your presence revives me and
Makes me whole again.
My limbs regain their strength and I stand upright,
I am no longer weak.
I feel the fear and anxiety retreating,
I feel my life returning.
Thank you, Lord Jesus, for staying close to me.
Thank you for being my friend.

Psalm 64

Lord God, architect of all creation,
Your land is suffering.
All that you have created is in want
And about to die.
The life that you have breathed into us
Is being burned away.
Your people are suffering and every living
Thing is drying up. Lord, we need rain.
I know you can see the entire picture from
Creation to eternity at a glance,
And you know what we need and when we need it,
But, Lord, we can't see the entire picture.
All we see are our crops dying,
Our livestock and even the wild game starving.
What can we do, Lord, but trust in you, you who
Watches over us from birth to death.
We know, Lord, that we waste the wonderful
Gifts you give us and don't use them wisely.
When we experience the abundant life
We don't think to thank you.
We puff out our chests and say, "How great I am."
"Look what I have done."
We forget what you have done for us and

What you do constantly.
Forgive us, Lord, forgive us and have mercy,
Forgive us, Lord, and send rain.

Psalm 65

I praise your name, Lord Jesus Christ.
I praise your name and give you thanks.
I thank you for all you have done for us, but
Especially for revealing yourself to us.
I hate to think what my life would be like
Without knowing you.
You came to us so long ago it is a miracle
That I know you at all, but I grew up in a
Family that knew you, and I was bathed in your love.
My parents, grandparents, aunts and uncles were
So loving and affirming of me, that when I heard
About you, I knew you were made in their image.
It was much later that I learned that they were
Made in Your image, and were doing
What you told them to do.
What a wonderful plan. We pass on our knowledge of you
To our children and grandchildren. We love them
As you love us. We support them as you support us,
So that they might be strong
And feel confident about themselves.
That is what you want us to do in your church,
Is it not, Lord?
You want us to love and strengthen everybody

So they will know you through us.
What a wonderful plan. It just might work.
I praise your wisdom, Lord, my God.

Psalm 66

Lord God of the universe, creator of all there is,
How can you stand the pain?
Somewhere today some of those
You love are rejoicing
Because they have killed and maimed
Another group of those you love.
Now those who were injured are searching for
The killers to avenge the killings.
This has happened over and over again,
And frequently in your name.
Your precious, wonderful creations are destroying
One another, and feeling justified in their action.
Why do we do this? Why do we hate what you
Have so beautifully created?
Can't we see how it must offend you,
And separate us from you?
We insult you daily because of our actions.
Lord have Mercy, Christ have mercy, Lord have mercy.
Lord, hear our prayer.

Psalm 67

rantor of all that is good,
I praise your name.
As I think of all that you have done for me
I thank you and I praise your name.
My entire life has been blessed
Because of you,
And I feel your presence wherever I go.
One of the places I go that pleases me very much
Occurs every Fall.
I start early before your new sun appears.
It is very quiet.
After thanking you for the rest of the night,
I venture out into the darkness.
As I climb into my selected position
I praise your name and thank you for your creation.
Then I watch and wait for your new day,
And I feel your presence.
Soon I hear some of your other creatures awaken,
And watch your sun push away the darkness.
Then comes the best part, your other creatures
Begin to appear.
First the sparrows and song birds. Then the
Cottontails and squirrels.

Then if I am lucky, the most magnificent of
All your wildlife, the white-tailed deer.
Silently, and cautiously, it moves out of the woods
And into the clearing. What a sight.
I thank you Lord for all your creation,
But especially for the white-tailed deer.

Psalm 68

ord God, our Governor and creator
Of land and sea,
How wonderful you are.
You have not only filled the forest with wild game,
You have also filled the sea with fish.
Wonderful fish that are not only good to eat,
But they are fun to catch.
Even if we are unsuccessful at catching fish,
It is wonderful just to be fishing.
One cannot be in a trout stream, on a lake,
Or on the sea without knowing you are there.
Your presence is felt in the mighty water if it is
Rushing past me or smooth as glass.
The excitement of feeling a pull on the line is
Surpassed only by knowing that
The fish has taken a big bite and I have
Successfully set the hook.
If I can then get the fish into my net,
My joy is complete.
What a wonderful gift you have given us, Lord.
You have provided food and a joyful way
To bring it to our table.

Thank you Lord for your many gifts, but especially
Thank you for fish and fishing.

Psalm 69

ll knowledge and intelligence are yours,
Lord God, but I have just discovered
Something you have known forever:
That fiendish Satan has usurped and destroyed
Many of those you love by
Invading one of the most honorable institutions
In this your world.
He has permitted and even aided certain
Successes of endeavor which
Have caused many of us to assume greatness
Only to suddenly take away all our
Hard earned skills, leaving us embarrassed
To the point of becoming hostile and profane.
Not only that, just when we are about to desert him
He returns our skills to us again.
Over and over again he uses this ploy, only to
Destroy us once more.
We have been known to take your
Name in vain and deny your existence.
I have finally seen the light, Lord, but
I can't speak for the others.
You have my solemn promise, Lord,
I will never play golf again.

Psalm 70

Lord Jesus, I have read what you have said
In Holy Scripture,
"Render unto Caesar what is Caesar's and
Render unto God what is God's."
Those of us who know you well understand
That all there is belongs to you,
And you are letting us use it while we
Are living here, and we
Presume that since we take nothing
With us, we will have no
Further need for it where we are going.
We are having a problem, Lord.
Some of those you love have mistaken money
And power for you.
Many of them don't know you, and that is
Our problem. However, many of them
Know you well, but have become ensnared in
The web of the evil one who has
Convinced them that if they have enough money
And power, they can be like you.
They are not only the gangsters and criminals.
Some of the leaders of our large corporations
And holders of high political office

Are guilty also. We need your help.
We will pray for them daily, Lord Jesus.
They need your help, as does your world.

Psalm 71

Provider of life and Creator of all things,
I praise your name in joy and thanksgiving
For the life you have given me. It has been
Long and exciting and seen many changes.
I particularly want to thank you for letting
Me live long enough to see all the changes.
I have learned a great deal in your gentle
School of experience.
Often the schooling was not so gentle
Because of my resistance,
But I bear no serious scars from the
Learning exercise.
I especially want to thank you for letting me
Live long enough to see through some of the
Misconceptions of my youth. I am sure there
Will come a time when we will understand
Everything, but it is comforting to know now
That my value is not measured by the
Material things I accumulate.
I know now that I am worthy because
Of your love for and acceptance of me.
My worth is not measured by the mark I
Leave on this world, but by

Allowing you to work through me and
Spreading the joy of that relationship.
It is not important that I be remembered,
But it is important that you are known
Because of something that I might have
Done or said.
I have not known these things always, Lord,
Even though they must have been said to me.
Thank you again, Lord, and I praise your name
For letting me hear them at last.

Psalm 72

In February 1946 Frances and I were married. In January 1996 she caught me looking at a little pretty thing made of diamonds and sapphires. I was told in no uncertain terms that I should not spend any money on that sort of thing. I wanted to do something special for the occasion, so I wrote a psalm of thanksgiving.

y God and most gracious heavenly father,
How great you are.
You have given me many wonderful gifts
Over my lifetime, and
I thank you for them.
Daily in my prayers I enumerate your gifts
And praise your name as their grantor.
Your generosity is beyond belief and your
Treasury of wonderful gifts is never empty.
The gift of life itself and of baptism which
Makes me part of your family
Are without doubt the most precious of all
Your gifts and are irreplaceable,
But there is one other gift, while maybe not as
Dramatic and earth-shaking,
That comes very close to producing the
Same degree of gratitude.

Fifty years ago, which is an *augenblick*
In your perception, you gave me
A mate who has made the life you have given me
Wonderful beyond belief.
She has been a loyal companion, a steadfast
Supporter, an uncompromising advocate
As well as an exciting lover, an unselfish mother
Of our children, and a creative homemaker.
She is not only a beautiful person, she
Is beautiful inside also.
She loves me dearly, but not only that,
She loves you dearly also.
Thank you, Lord God, for Frances,
You could not have done any better.